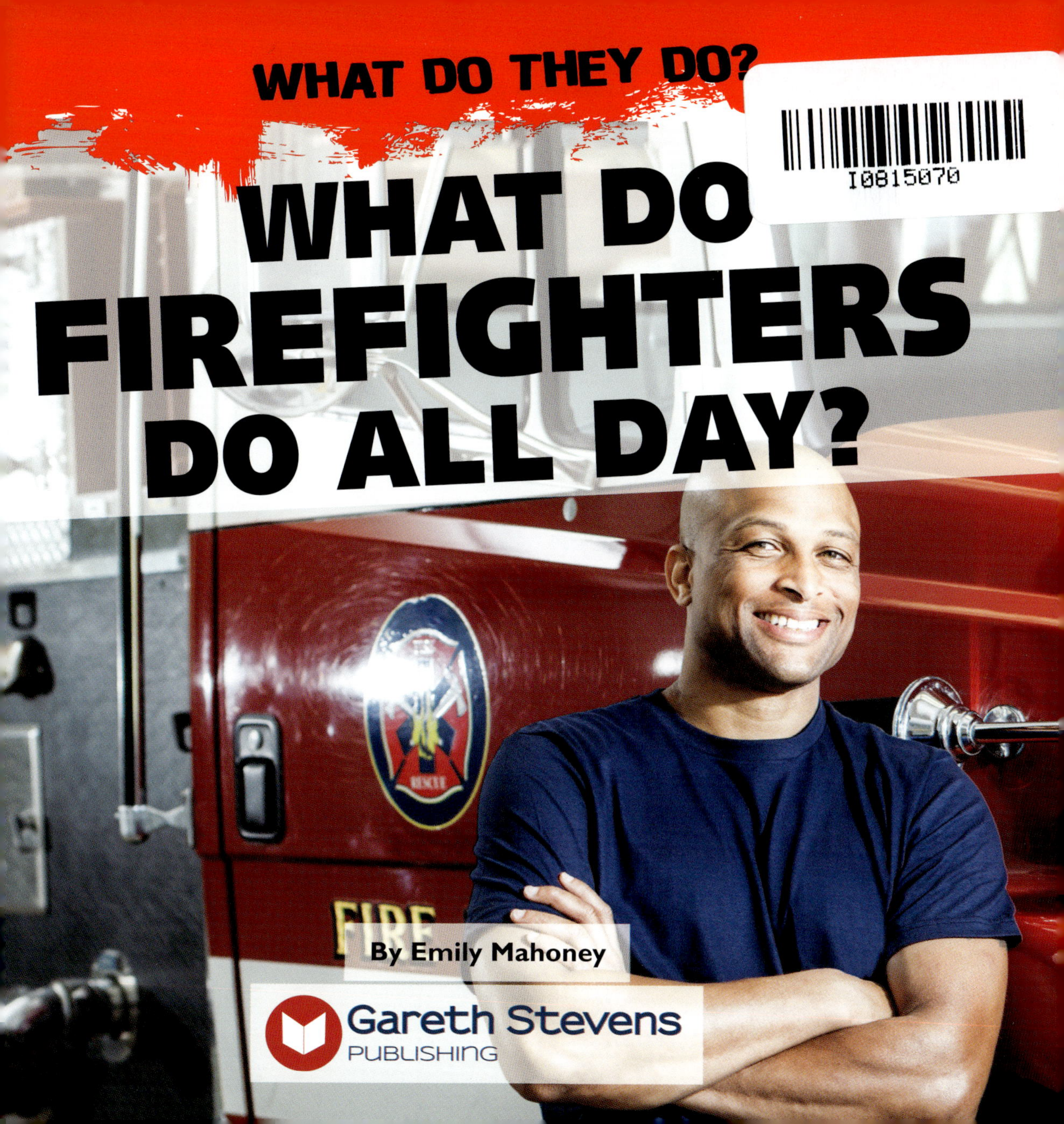
WHAT DO THEY DO?
WHAT DO
FIREFIGHTERS
DO ALL DAY?
I0815070
FIRE
By Emily Mahoney
Gareth Stevens
PUBLISHING

Please visit our website, www.garethstevens.com. For a free color catalog of all our high-quality books, call toll free 1-800-542-2595 or fax 1-877-542-2596.

Library of Congress Cataloging-in-Publication Data

Names: Mahoney, Emily Jankowski, author.
Title: What do firefighters do all day? / Emily Mahoney.
Description: New York : Gareth Stevens Publishing, [2021] | Series: What do they do? | Includes index.
Identifiers: LCCN 2019054540 | ISBN 9781538256732 (library binding) | ISBN 9781538256718 (paperback) | ISBN 9781538256725 (6 Pack)| ISBN 9781538256749 (ebook)
Subjects: LCSH: Fire fighters—Juvenile literature.
Classification: LCC HD8039.F5 M34 2020 | DDC 628.9/2023—dc23
LC record available at https://lccn.loc.gov/2019054540

Published in 2021 by
Gareth Stevens Publishing
111 East 14th Street, Suite 349
New York, NY 10003

Editor: Emily Mahoney
Designer: Laura Bowen

Photo credits: Series art Dima Polies/Shutterstock.com; cover, pp. 1, 5 kali9/E+/Getty Images; p. 7 JBryson/iStock/Getty Images Plus/Getty Images; p. 9 Tom Carter/Photolibrary/Getty Images Plus/Getty Images; p. 11 Maskot/Maskot/Getty Images; p. 13 Daniel Barry/Stringer/Getty Images News/Getty Images; p. 15 Chris Cheadle/Photographer's Choice/Getty Images Plus/Getty Images; p. 17 Viviane Moos/Contributor/Corbis Historical/Getty Images; p. 19 kdshutterman/iStock/Getty Images Plus/Getty Images; p. 21 LPETTET/E+/Getty Images.

Printed in the United States of America

Some of the images in this book illustrate individuals who are models. The depictions do not imply actual situations or events.

CPSIA compliance information: Batch #CS20GS: For further information contact Gareth Stevens, New York, New York, at 1-800-542-2595.

CONTENTS

Boldface words appear in the glossary.

Helping the Community

Being a firefighter is a **dangerous** job, but it's very **rewarding**. Firefighters must put their own life at **risk** to help members of their community. But not every day is filled with big fires. Read on to find out exactly what a firefighter does during their day.

Planning and Training

When firefighters aren't putting out fires, they commonly spend their time working at the firehouse. They often work on training exercises with other firefighters to keep their skills sharp and to stay in shape. They must be fit to lift heavy hoses!

Firefighters need to be ready to take a call as soon as it comes in. This means always making sure that their equipment, or gear, is clean, stocked, and working well. They also need to make sure that their fire truck is clean and full of gas in case they get a call.

VOLUNTEER

Getting a Call

When a call comes in that someone needs help, firefighters must be quick to act. They may have only a few minutes! Firefighters put on their gear, including a **fireproof** suit and boots, a helmet, and eye **protection**. Then they jump in the truck to go to help.

Not every call is a big fire. Firefighters also **respond** to calls about small fires, people who are hurt, and even **chemical** spills that need to be cleaned up. Every call is different. A firefighter must be ready to check the scene to see how they can help best.

Big Fires

Sometimes, firefighters do get called to battle a building on fire. When that happens, the firefighters first see if there is anyone in the building who needs help. Then, they make a plan to put out the fire in the fastest way they can.

Firefighters commonly fix their fire hoses to fire hydrants. This is how they get the water needed to spray the fire to put it out. Many firefighters often work at the same time to do this. They also need to watch for signs that the building **structure** is becoming weaker. It could fall and hurt someone.

CHANDUR HASSO
F.D.N.Y.
FIRE

After the Call

Once a fire has been put out, firefighters still have work to do. Every call must be **documented**. All of their gear must be inspected, or checked, and the gear must be returned to the fire truck so it's ready for the next call.

A Heroic Job

Even though it's a hard and dangerous job, a firefighter saves lives. They train, keep their gear clean and ready, and go out on calls to help people. A firefighter never knows what their day will be like! One thing is for sure, though: Firefighters are heroes in their community.

ENGINEER
FIREFIGHTER
CAPTAIN

GLOSSARY

chemical: matter that can be mixed with other matter to cause changes

dangerous: unsafe

document: to write down for official proof

fireproof: not able to be burned

protection: the act of keeping people from harm

respond: to have a reaction to something

rewarding: producing a good feeling that you have done something important or helpful

risk: the possibility that something bad or unsafe could happen

structure: the parts that make up a building

FOR MORE INFORMATION

BOOKS

Aylmore, Angela. *We Work at the Fire Station.* Chicago, IL: Heinemann Library, 2006.

Grambling, Lois G. *My Mom Is a Firefighter.* New York, NY: Scholastic, 2007.

WEBSITES

Fire Safe Kids

www.firesafekids.org/

This website has fun activities and helpful information about fire safety for kids.

NVFC National Junior Firefighter

juniors.nvfc.org/juniors/

Learn more about the junior firefighter program.

INDEX